THE LAND AND RESOURCES OF TEXAS

Shaping the Growth of the State

Isabelle Marfa

PowerKiDS press

NEW YORK

Published in 2010 by The Rosen Publishing Group, Inc.
29 East 21st Street, New York, NY 10010

Book Design: Michael J. Flynn

Photo Credits: Cover (wind turbines, corn), cover, pp. 3, 4, 6, 10, 16, 18, 20, 24, 26, 28, 30, 31, 32 (Texas emblem on all), back cover (Texas flag), 3–32 (textured background), 6 (prairie, Guadalupe River), 7 (Lake Travis, cotton field, grassland), 9 (corn, onions), 10 (cattle), 11 (bull), 14 (barbed wire), 15 (sheep), 16 (mill), 17 (creek), 19 (open pit mine), 25 (wind turbines), 26 (house), 27 (solar panels), 29 (globe) Shutterstock.com; pp. 4 (map), 12 (map), 22 (map) © GeoAtlas; pp. 8 (cotton gin), 13 (cowboys and cattle) Leonard McCombe/Time & Life Pictures/Getty Images; p. 15 (goats) Tim Graham/ Getty Images; pp. 20 (workers), 21 (Lucas Gusher, Spindletop) Getty Images; p. 23 (oil field) Shel Hershorn/Hulton Archive/Getty Images.

Library of Congress Cataloging-in-Publication Data

Marfa, Isabelle.
  The land and resources of Texas : shaping the growth of the state / Isabelle Marfa.
       p. cm. — (Spotlight on Texas)
  Includes index.
  ISBN 978-1-61532-478-1 (pbk.)
  ISBN 978-1-61532-479-8 (6-pack)
  ISBN 978-1-61532-480-4 (library binding)
  1. Natural resources—Texas—Juvenile literature. 2. Economic development—Texas—Juvenile literature. 3. Texas—Economic conditions—Juvenile literature. I. Title.
  HC107.T4M37 2010
  333.709764—dc22
                                   2009033232

Manufactured in the United States of America

CPSIA Compliance Information: Batch # WW1ORC: For further information contact Rosen Publishing, New York, New York at 1-800-237-9932.

CONTENTS

TEXAS: LAND OF NATURAL RESOURCES

Texas is the second-largest state in the United States in both size and population. It has four major land regions, or areas, that have mountains, plains, valleys, hills, rivers, canyons, forests, and deserts. It also has many **natural resources** such as oil, natural gas, coal, lumber, rivers, rich soil, **minerals**, rainfall, sun, and wind.

In this book, we'll look at how Texas's land and resources have shaped its growth.

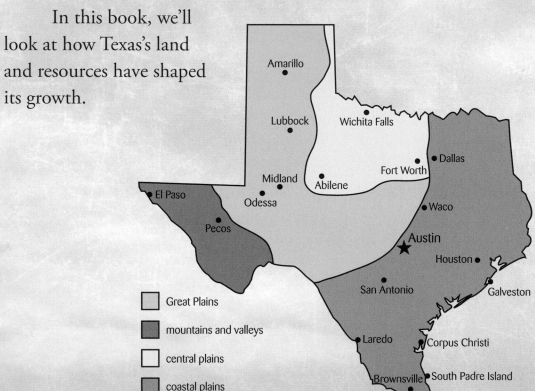

Amarillo

Lubbock   Wichita Falls

Dallas

Midland   Fort Worth

El Paso   Abilene

Odessa

Pecos   Waco

Austin

Houston

San Antonio   Galveston

Great Plains

mountains and valleys   Laredo   Corpus Christi

central plains

Brownsville   South Padre Island

coastal plains

LAND REGIONS OF TEXAS

	Coastal Plains	Central Plains	Great Plains	Mountains and Valleys
Features	flat, low, forests, rivers	hills, grasslands, hardwood trees	flat, few trees, canyons (steep valleys)	mountains, valleys, deserts, rivers
Weather Conditions	hot, lots of moisture in the air, lots of rainfall	dry air, good rainfall	dry air, hot in summer and cold in winter, regular rainfall	very dry air, hot, little rainfall
Resources	forests of pine and hardwood, coal, minerals, wind, sun	minerals, rich soil	some trees, wildlife, wind, sun	pine forests, grasses
Economy	farming, fishing, ranching, lumbering, mining, oil, gas, manufacturing, wind farms, solar plants	fruit and vegetable farming, ranching, oil and gas, coal	cotton and wheat farming, ranching, oil and gas, wind farms, solar plants	cotton, fruit and vegetable farming, ranching, coal, oil and gas
Large Cities	Austin, Houston, San Antonio, Dallas	Fort Worth, Abilene, Wichita Falls	Lubbock, Midland, Amarillo	El Paso, Pecos

AGRICULTURE

Texas's land has shaped its **agricultural** and **economic** growth from the first settlements to the present day. Farmers make the best use of the different areas' natural features, soil, and water.

Farming was done on a small scale in the 1700s and early 1800s. Farms were set up in and around the Spanish **missions** and small communities.

prairie

Guadalupe River

6

In 1821, Mexico— which included Texas—gained independence from Spain. The Mexican government gave people land in Texas to get them to move there. As more settlers came, farms grew larger to produce more food. American settlers in Texas used the **plantation** system for growing cotton. The system depended on the work of slaves. This led to more settlement.

Lake Travis

grassland

cotton field

Many of Texas's natural features make it a good place to grow crops.

The **American Civil War** was over in 1865, ending slavery. However, cotton was still an important crop. Plantations were broken into smaller farms. Plantation owners rented the land to farmers for money or a share of their crops.

The 1880s brought new farming methods and new crops. Businesses made and sold farm machinery and supplies. Others made goods such as cottonseed oil and plant food. These businesses created more jobs, and the population increased.

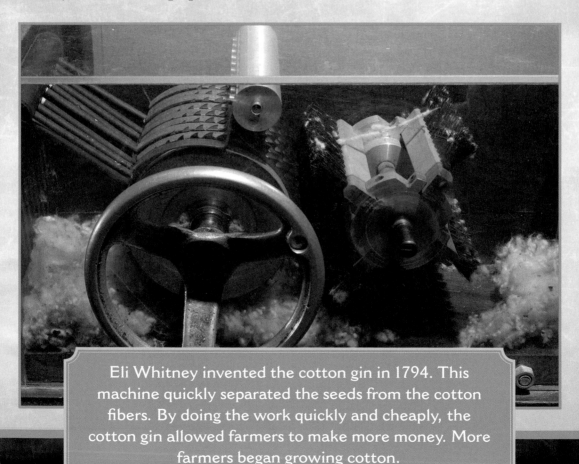

Eli Whitney invented the cotton gin in 1794. This machine quickly separated the seeds from the cotton fibers. By doing the work quickly and cheaply, the cotton gin allowed farmers to make more money. More farmers began growing cotton.

Agriculture continues to be an important part of the Texas economy. Texas grows about 200 food and nonfood crops such as wheat, oats, corn, rice, beans, peanuts, onions, tomatoes, oranges, beets, cotton, and flowers.

corn

onions

Corn and onions are just two Texas crops that are grown using natural methods.

Natural Farming

Today, natural farming is big business in Texas. Texas became a leader in practicing farming that uses natural methods, instead of man-made goods that can harm nature, to control pests and feed plants.

RANCHING

The Spanish brought cattle, sheep, goats, and horses to America for food, clothing, and riding. The open grasslands of Texas are ideal for raising farm animals. The animals wandered the grassy plains, where they had a steady food supply. Their numbers increased. By the early 1800s, the missions were no longer the center of Texas life. Settlers began to capture and herd the animals. They started to raise animals as a business. The population grew as people came to Texas to ranch.

Raising cattle for beef is a big part of today's Texas economy.

Look at Those Horns!

Longhorn cattle got their name from their long horns. Their horns can be up to 4 feet (1.2 m) from tip to tip! Longhorn cattle are a combination of cattle brought to Texas by the Spanish and the English. Because they're strong, they can live in hot or cold weather, eat many different kinds of plants, and go for several days without water. Ranchers mixed longhorns with other cattle to create new stock.

During the Civil War, cattle weren't moved to northern markets. After the war, the population in northern cities grew. Many people wanted beef. Ranchers hired cowboys for cattle drives. Cowboys herded and looked after large numbers of cattle on the trails. Cattle drives moved cattle to markets that were far away. The drives were often long, hard, and full of danger.

Cattle drives became a way of life in Texas. Goods and services were needed by people on the trails. Towns were built. The population and economy grew.

The Chisholm Trail was about 1,000 miles (1,600 km) long. The trail went from San Antonio, Texas, to the railroad in Abilene, Kansas. It was the most used cattle trail until about 1871, when more railroads and other trails appeared.

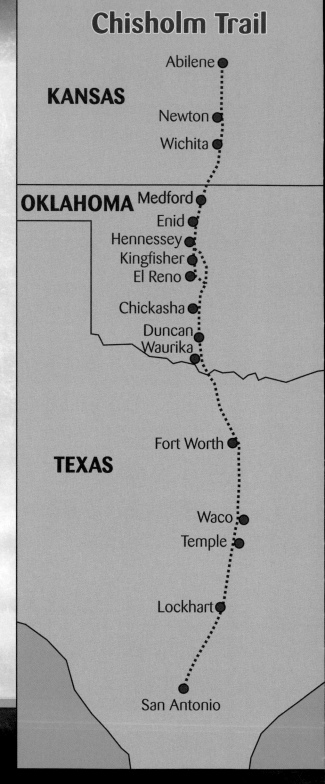

Chisholm Trail

KANSAS
- Abilene
- Newton
- Wichita

OKLAHOMA
- Medford
- Enid
- Hennessey
- Kingfisher
- El Reno
- Chickasha
- Duncan
- Waurika

TEXAS
- Fort Worth
- Waco
- Temple
- Lockhart
- San Antonio

Cowboys rode on horseback, herding cattle on the trails and across the open land.

A Spanish Cowboy

The first planned Texas cattle drive was in 1779. At that time, the Spanish were fighting the British along the Gulf of Mexico coast. Spanish leader General Bernardo de Galvez sent Francisco Garcia into Texas for food supplies. Local ranchers in San Antonio gathered up almost 2,000 cattle. Garcia led a drive to get the cattle to New Orleans. Some say this cattle drive, planned by a Spanish cowboy, was the beginning of cattle trade between Texas and Louisiana.

Open-range ranching and cattle drives caused problems between ranchers and farmers. Many argued over land rights. Some farmers didn't want cattle getting into their crops. Ranchers didn't want their cattle to become ill from other cattle. Farmers and ranchers often used wood, stone, or thorny plants to mark the borders of their land. However, building fences with these things took time and didn't always work.

The 1874 invention of barbed wire changed ranching and farming. Good fences could be set up quickly around both large and small areas of land. New businesses, methods, and goods for farming and ranching appeared. Cattle were fed grains instead of feeding on open grasslands.

Today, new and improved methods have kept ranching a major part of the Texas economy.

barbed wire

goats

sheep

Sheep and goat ranchers use mesh and wire fences instead of barbed wire. These fences don't harm the animal's wool and hair.

LUMBERING

By the mid-1800s, lumber companies had cut down many forests in the northeastern United States. The wood was used for building and fuel.

The companies went west and south looking for new lumber supplies. They came to Texas as railroads were built farther into the state. The companies brought people and jobs. Lumber camps were set up, and wood and paper mills were constructed. Communities grew up around the new businesses. Lumber became important to the growth of Texas. It continues to provide a large part of the state's economy.

The wood pulp, or smashed wood, from this mill in east Texas will be used to make many different paper products.

In the early 1900s, Texas state government made rules for cutting and moving trees. They also made rules about the methods used by wood and paper mills and by the makers of lumber goods. Tree farms began to replant trees for future use and to guard existing forests.

State and U.S. forest services manage large areas of Texas forests. This is a picture of Big Creek flowing through a forest in Brazos Bend State Park.

COAL MINING

In the 1800s, people came from far away to work in Texas's coal mines. Coal was an important **energy** supply. It was used for heat. Coal was also used to fuel trains and boats.

At first, coal was mined in small underground mines. As the need for coal increased, strip or surface mining was used. More and more mining camps were built. These camps grew into towns. Stores, factories, warehouses, and businesses started. Many areas of Texas grew, and the economy grew as well.

Today, mining is still an important part of the Texas economy. Minerals and metals such as iron, clay, salt, sand, stone, silver, and gold are also mined.

This is a picture of a surface mine. Today, Texas is one of the top five producers of coal in the United States. The coal business is using science and technology to discover ways to make coal and coal mining less harmful to Earth.

BLACK GOLD!

The natural resource that's had perhaps the greatest effect on shaping the growth and economy of Texas is oil, or petroleum. It has become so valued that it's called black gold! Some Texas oil wells were discovered by chance when farmers, ranchers, and businessmen dug wells for water. Instead, they found oil.

In the late 1800s, oil companies began moving into east Texas to drill for oil. The companies brought tools and workers. At first, the wells they drilled didn't produce much oil. Many men left. Patillo Higgins believed there was a great deal of oil in the coastal plains. He bought land in Beaumont, Texas. Spindletop Hill was on the land. In 1893, he hired a man named Anthony Lucas to begin drilling. After oil gushed from the well at Spindletop in 1901, more wells were drilled.

This 1901 picture shows workers drilling at Spindletop.

Lucas drilled on Spindletop for over 8 years. The Spindletop well, called the Lucas Gusher, struck oil on January 10, 1901. By 1903, there were over 400 wells on Spindletop.

Lucas Gusher

Spindletop

The wells at Spindletop and other places produced a great deal of oil. Pipes were connected from individual locations to increase the amount of oil carried to **refineries**. The oil was made into goods such as heating oil, waxes, creams, automobile fuel, and plant food. Newer and bigger refineries were built. New petroleum companies formed. Cities grew larger as businesses that supplied, serviced, and manufactured petroleum goods grew. The economy of Texas became stronger from the oil, the goods made from it, and the businesses connected to it.

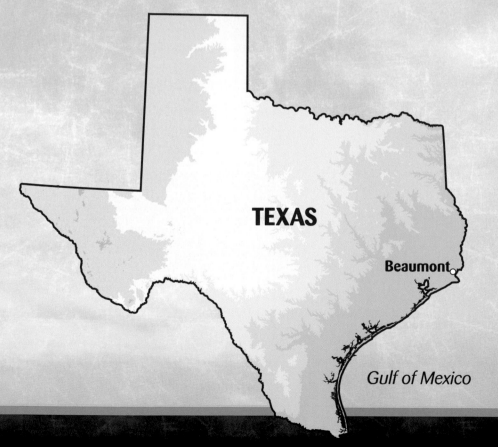

TEXAS

Beaumont

Gulf of Mexico

Beaumont, Texas, is near the Gulf of Mexico. Today, oil companies drill for oil in the gulf as well as on the land. Here you can see a large oil field in the Gulf of Mexico.

WIND ★ ENERGY

Wind energy is one of the fastest-growing businesses for producing electricity in the world today. Texas is a national leader in making, using, and selling wind energy. It's also a leader in studying the best ways to store the energy produced. Hundreds of wind **turbines** in Texas are adding millions of dollars to its economy.

Many farmers, ranchers, and oilmen have wind turbines on their land. Wind can't be used up. It doesn't need to be replanted, mined, or moved. Wind-produced electricity is clean energy—it doesn't pollute the land, water, or air.

In Texas, the production of wind energy has created many jobs—from planning and constructing turbines, plants, and power lines to the creation of new businesses and services.

This is a wind farm near White Deer, Texas.
The turbines change moving wind into electricity.
The electricity is then sent over power lines.

SOLAR ENERGY

Many people believe another Texas resource—the sun—should be used to produce clean energy, too! Texas, especially western Texas, gets a great deal of sunlight.

Scientists have found ways to capture the sun's energy in **solar cells**. Solar energy can be used to produce electricity. Electricity created from solar energy lessens energy costs. The sale of the electricity to other areas of the country means economic growth for Texas.

Solar cells can be used to provide power for single homes like the one pictured here.

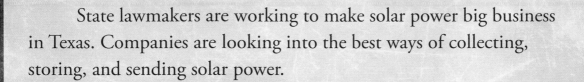

State lawmakers are working to make solar power big business in Texas. Companies are looking into the best ways of collecting, storing, and sending solar power.

These solar cells are part of a solar power plant. Solar energy plants have many solar cells that collect and change solar power into electricity. The electricity is used by many businesses and communities.

Going Forward

Texas has used its many resources—good soil, grasslands, lumber, coal, and oil—to successfully build its communities and wealth. Today, Texas and its economy continue to grow through clean energy—wind and solar power. Texas is a leader in creating and using methods that provide energy without polluting Earth.

Growth of Texas from Its Land and Resources

- mission and community
- farms

1600s

- coal mining
- farm animals raised as a business

EARLY 1800s

- ranching and cattle drives
- lumbering

MID–TO LATE 1800s

Texas

The land and resources of Texas have shaped its growth and its importance in the world.

- oil drilling

- wind and solar power

LATE 1800S – EARLY 1900S

LATE 1900S

READER RESPONSE PROJECTS

- Choose a natural resource you read about in this book. Use what you have read, as well as additional facts from the Internet, to list reasons why it's important to the growth of Texas.

- Write a newspaper article on the land region of Texas you feel has had the most effect on its growth. Include facts about the area's resources and how they shaped settlement and economic activity.

- Use the Internet and other sources to gather information about the different methods and materials used in natural farming. Create a poster displaying interesting facts about natural farming.

- Using pictures and charts, create a poster that shows how the population and economic growth in Texas was shaped by its land and resources.

GLOSSARY

agricultural (aa-grih-KUHL-chuh-ruhl) Having to do with farming.

American Civil War (uh-MEHR-uh-kuhn SIH-vuhl WOHR) A war (1861–1865) between the North and South in the United States.

economic (eh-kuh-NAH-mihk) Having to do with the movement of money and goods.

energy (EH-nuhr-jee) Power.

mineral (MIH-nuh-ruhl) Something found in nature that is not living.

mission (MIH-shun) A place where people work to spread their beliefs.

natural resource (NA-chuh-ruhl REE-sohrs) Something such as minerals, forests, water, and land that is found in nature and can be used by people.

plantation (plan-TAY-shun) A large farm where crops are grown.

refinery (rih-FY-nuh-ree) A place where something is made into a more pure form.

solar cell (SOH-luhr SEHL) A tool that changes energy from the sun into electricity.

turbine (TUHR-byn) An engine with blades that makes energy by spinning.

INDEX

Due to the changing nature of Internet links, the Rosen Publishing Group, Inc., has developed an online list of Web sites related to the subject of this book. This site is updated regularly. Please use this link to access the list: **http://www.rcbmlinks.com/sot/landre/**